CONCRETE POOL BUYERS' GUIDE

Everything you need to know about buying a concrete pool: choosing a builder, quoting, design, types, features, cost

by Steve Nener and Robin Bower

The Water's Edge Pool Design and Landscaping

CONCRETE POOL BUYERS' GUIDE

Copyright © 2015 RB Publishing

www.thewatersedge.com.au

ISBN: 978-0-9941913-1-1

CONTENTS

Introduction

Thanks so much for taking the time to visit our website and for reading this pool buyers' guide. We've worked with hundreds of clients for more than 30 years selling and building all types of pools in the industry so we have a very good idea of what people want to know when they buy a pool.

First up, we design and build concrete and vinyl pools. We will talk about other types of pools; just know that we recommend concrete pools. There are plenty of resources available to find out about fibreglass and aboveground pools.

So, according to our expertise and our clients' queries, we've tried to answer the most frequently asked questions. Here they are:

1. **How do I choose my pool builder/designer?**

2. **What kind of pool should I buy?**

3. **How do you build a concrete pool?**

4. **What features should I consider?**

5. **How do I know if it's a fair price?**

We really hope that reading through the answers to these questions will inform your buying and give you the confidence to choose the right pool for you so that you can be assured of many years of enjoyment with your pool.

What to do before you start

As with anything, it's a good idea to have some information about what you're buying so you can compare products, know industry terminology and show that you are not a complete novice. We recommend that you do some research before contacting a pool builder. Having some ideas about your **wish list** will give him (it is usually a 'him'!) some background information and a good start on designing what you want. We know that you want to hear his recommendations (after all you do have to pay for that!) but he will still come up with ideas; these ideas will work better with how he perceives your own needs and lifestyle requirements.

To help you plan what will go into your space, collect photographs of what others have done with the features that you admire. Start a **scrapbook** of ideas. Showing this to your pool builder will really help him visualise what you are thinking, and you can work out what will stay and what will go based on other factors. Your spending expectations are an important factor.

You will need to consider what **shape and type** of pool you want. The type of pool can be a choice of aboveground, concrete, vinyl or fibreglass. There are advantages and disadvantages in all types. The shape will depend mostly on your space, especially if you have a small unusually shaped area. The area may determine the shape. If you have a large area, you can have any shape you wish, so you will need to consider how you want to use the pool and what sort of look you are after. Have a look at some examples of the different styles available in our gallery.

Another aspect you need to consider is the **weather**. In most of Australia, we are lucky to have hot dry summers so protection from rain is not so much of an issue. However, you may want a heated pool so you can swim all year round and therefore need an enclosure to protect you from the rain. You may also want to consider an indoor pool if the weather is a real issue in your area.

Think about how you will **use** your pool. Do you have young children who are learning to swim, love diving and frolicking in the pool? Are you an older couple who just want to enjoy a quick dip and a drink by the pool? Do you love swimming laps? A standard pool size is 1–1.8 metres deep and there should be a gradual slope to the deep end. Your use of the pool will determine its shape and size so think about this early.

You can certainly get your wish list ready but be prepared to adjust this according to your **budget** and size of your area. Aboveground pools are the lowest in cost followed by fibreglass, vinyl and finally concrete. You should have a budget in mind and let the pool builder know so that he can adapt the products and features to suit.

Be prepared to face some **long-term costs** when it comes to pool maintenance.

However, by carefully choosing products, you can minimise this cost. Do some research on this or ask your pool builder.

Get an idea about your **council's building codes** and allowances. Your pool builder will usually liaise with them for you but gather information so you don't get any surprises.

Contact your **insurance company** to find out about extra insurance costs that may be required when you get a pool. All pool builders who are members of the Swimming Pool and Spa Association have indemnity insurance.

Be familiar with the **features** that are available so you can factor them into your wish list, scrapbook and ideas for the total design.

Try to be as **energy efficient** as you can. This means doing some research on pool appliances that have good energy ratings, pool covers to save water evaporation, timers, preventative maintenance and lowering the temperature of the pool heater when not in use.

There are energy-efficient pool pumps on the market that can reduce power consumption significantly.

Most pool builders will do an initial site visit as a free consultation.

A **pool designer** will design your entire outdoor landscape to maximise the potential of your property while seamlessly blending your style choices. If you want the best investment for your pool, you should consider a pool designer.

We will talk about the questions you need to ask but the pool designer will also ask you some questions so you need to be prepared for these.

Some of his questions may be:

- How long have you been looking for a pool?
- Have you been to a display centre to get ideas?
- Do you know the difference between fibreglass and concrete?
- Do you want a concrete or a fibreglass pool?
- How would you like to use your pool?

This guide will help you organise your ideas and have some answers ready.

Now to your questions...

Q1. What type of pool should I buy?

The main choice a buyer must make is what type of pool to buy. **Aboveground pools** can be assembled fairly quickly and are inexpensive but are limited in how they can enhance your home. **Fibreglass pools** are manufactured in pre-made shapes so if you have a large area, want a regular shape, and want to keep the costs low, some would choose a fibreglass pool. However, you may struggle to find a shape that suits your specific needs.

Vinyl pools are constructed of brick and have a thick vinyl liner placed on the inside of the pool. These are a good alternative to concrete pools as they can be custom built to suit a backyard but are generally less expensive than concrete pools.

Concrete pools are customised to suit your particular needs. They can be a unique shape — a pool that you will not ever see anywhere else and that is completely suited to your backyard and lifestyle. Concrete pools are robust and will last for 20 years or more if looked after well.

The added features can also be worked into the design to suit any use of the pool. In this case, a pool designer can enhance and add value to your home by creating a beautiful outdoor environment.

Once you've considered which type of pool to buy, you need to decide on whether to have a **chlorinated (manual or automatic), saltwater** or **mineral systems** pool.

Manual chlorination

Traditionally, pools were hand chlorinated with granulated chlorine. Pool owners need to balance the pool water because this kills mould and bacteria in the pool. If the balance is not correct, people will complain about sore eyes and skin irritation.

Chemical monitoring and dosing

This computerised system tests the water chemistry every three to five minutes. It has special pumps to draw in the chlorine or acid if required to balance the pool.

Saltwater

These pools use dissolved salt instead of chlorine to clean and sanitise the pool water. Pool owners need to keep the pH level balanced regularly. After the initial dose of salt, however, amounts are added just to keep the balance. Saltwater pools are generally cheaper to maintain than chlorine pools and are more favourable to bathers.

Mineral systems

Mineral spas have been used for centuries for soothing the body and ensuring a healthy skin. Mineral systems for swimming pools use fewer chemicals which affect the body. Magnesium and potassium are used with a special filtration system that keeps the pool water clear and clean, and helps to detoxify the body.

Q2. How do I choose my pool builder/designer?

Let's assume you are armed with appropriate research and you are ready to contact a pool designer.

Here are some questions for you to ask your prospective pool designer:

How many pools have you built?

The most important factor when choosing someone to build your pool is experience. If the pool designer has many years' experience in the business, he will be familiar with every type of landscape, every type of challenge and be able to solve these with relative ease. You can then be assured of having the process flow as smoothly as possible.

If you are buying a custom-built concrete pool, the pool designer who has built many of these types of pools will not be daunted by a challenging site or its size.

Do you organise council approvals?

Find out if the pool designer will liaise with council over approvals (they normally do). Council approval could take some weeks so factor this in when scheduling.

Are you a member of any industry bodies?

A reputable pool designer will always be a member of their state Swimming Pool and Spa Association (SPASA) and the Housing Industry of Australia (HIA).

Can I see some examples of your work?

This should be mandatory and easy to view on the pool designer's website. Look for good workmanship, custom-built designs that suit the landscape, large and small projects, and a range of different features that you can include in your design.

Can I see some client references?

Client references and testimonials are critical to finding a reputable pool designer. These testimonials should be viewable on the pool designer's website. Ask your pool designer for more details if required.

What is included in the contract?

Once you've had a quote and you've requested a design which you're happy with, you are ready to sign the contract.

This is a legally binding document for both parties and you should read it carefully. Your contract should be supported by drawings which show the physical dimensions, size, shape, access and depth of the pool.

Your contract should show the schedule of progress payments with the amount and timings. Find out if variations are allowed on the contract as, if you change your mind midway, you could be liable to pay extra costs and the project may experience significant delays.

How long will it take to build my pool?

The length of time it takes from start to finish depends on a number of factors. These include the time taken at council submission stage, agreement on the design, any variations to the design, disruption by weather, amount of detail required in the design, size of the area and pool, if it's a renovation or a new project, pool fence installation and landscaping, and any other features that you have decided to include. For a new project, it generally takes between four and six months, depending on these factors.

If you want to be swimming by Christmas, you will need to have signed a contract in about August so start looking for your pool designer in June.

Q3. How do you build a concrete pool?

Once you've had a site visit, agreed on a design and signed the contract, you are ready to start the project.

These are the steps in the process:

Application to the Water Corporation

If the pool encroaches on to the minister's sewer (a conduit laid for the carriage of sewage or wastewater), extra costs will be incurred. A good pool designer knows this prior to project start. An application must be lodged with the Water Corporation at the start of the project.

Engineering

An engineer is commissioned to design the integrity of the swimming pool structure with regard to other possible elements such as boundary fences, house, sewerage, columns, elevations, and contours. This stage is critical to the integrity and safety of the site and a final report is used for submitting to council.

Pool fencing

In Australia, it is a requirement for council to have a fencing contractor supply a site plan showing a pool fence designed to Australian standards.

Site visit

A site visit is undertaken to determine the finished pool levels. Excavation can then be carried out.

Excavation

This is when a bobcat comes onsite to dig the hole for the pool. The excavated material is transported offsite to another location. Generally, the cost overrun of excavation is determined by the tip fees. On a standard sandy level site and/or if hard material (limestone) is discovered, this will add significant cost to excavation. If the pool designer believes there is a chance of hitting hard material on the site, he has a duty of care to explain this possibility and any additional costs that may be incurred.

Pool filtration system

Before the main construction of the pool starts, the plumbing for the skimmer box needs to be installed, any pipes for water features, and cables for electrical elements such as the pool light. The plumbing is installed prior to concreting.

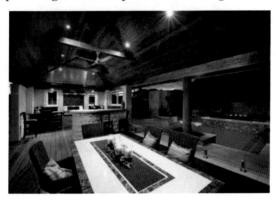

Formwork

Steel reinforcements are used to create the shape of the pool, as well as form the solid foundation that the pool requires for strength and integrity.

Concreting

Once the steelwork is completed, premixed concrete is sprayed into the structured hole and the pool really begins to take shape.

Plastering and acid wash

Plaster is applied to the pool walls and floor to create a smooth and durable finish. This is performed by highly skilled practitioners and requires good weather and continuous work. Once all surfaces are done, the pool takes 24 hours to dry. Acid washing is necessary to keep the surface clean and free from bacteria and algae. This involves scrubbing the pool with the acid mixture. Some products can be acid washed the following day to enhance the colour of the plaster.

Tiling

Most domestic pools only have part of the pool tiled, unlike large commercial pools which are usually fully tiled. Tiling can be expensive so it is wise to budget for the area you require. Mosaic tiles are an attractive option. These tiles come in two main styles — **ceramic mosaics** and **glass mosaics**. Mosaic tiles are generally under 100 mm in size and are supplied with a mesh backing to form a sheet of tiles (300 x 300 mm). These are premium tiles. A **waterline tile** is placed between the coping and the water. Most pool designers will supply this as a standard. The Australian standard is 200 x 200 mm.

Coping

Once the concreting is completed (between seven and 21 days), it is time to add the pool coping which is the edging placed around the top of the pool. It protects the structure from anything surrounding it and adds a nice aesthetic to the whole look. The coping can be natural stone, concrete pavers, clay pavers or brick.

Filling

A standard garden hose is used to fill the pool with scheme water. It takes 24 hours.

Completion and handover

When the pool is filled, the pool designer will carry out the chemical balance of the water and test all the filtering equipment and operations. Owners should then get a lesson in how to look after the pool, testing the chemicals, filtering, vacuuming and general maintenance.

Q4. What features should I consider?

When you buy a pool, you need to think about what goes around the pool. There are a number of features to consider.

Landscaping and plants

Pool designers will provide you with a design for the **'soft landscaping'**, i.e. advice on the plants you will need to surround your pool. Plants can have various uses: they can provide shade, protection from the wind, and screening from neighbours. They also make the environment look fantastic. The pool designer will know which plants are suitable for which environments, which ones drop leaves, and which ones have problematic root systems that are not advisable to use for pool areas. Some might even visit the garden centre with you to choose your plants.

If you have a **saltwater** pool, you will need to choose salt-tolerant plants that will not be poisoned by high levels of salt. Some good varieties are Chinese Hibiscus, rosemary, olive, cycads, palms and all species of agave (sometimes known as cactus).

Chlorinated pools need to be fed chemicals to kill any germs in the pool so you will need to have plants that are not going to be affected by these chemicals. The best plants for chlorinated pool areas are Star Jasmine, Mondo grass and Cordyline (with the beautiful purple leaves).

Avoid any plant variety that has a root system that can affect the structure of your pool over time. These are plants like the rubber tree, umbrella tree (and any ficus), as well as bamboos and melaleucas.

Decking

Timber decking adds a very professional ambience to your whole outdoor area. With timber, the choice is between **softwood** or **hardwood**. Hardwoods grow more slowly and are more dense so they are tougher and more expensive. They are long-wearing, pest resistant and require less maintenance. Softwoods are easier to work with and are more commonly used in construction. All types of wood need to be seasoned before construction and this takes longer for some wood than others.

Consider your location before deciding on the wood to use; if you are in a **bushfire** area, you will need a wood that complies to local fire safety codes.

You may also like to consider the **environmental** impact of the timber you choose (use of fuel in transporting the product or forest logging). You might also consider **recycled** timber which can be older and already seasoned.

There are several options provided by solid timber:

Blackbutt — great for a bushfire classified area as they are naturally fire resistant and durable

Cypress pine — a knotty timber that is good for use both inside and outside

Jarrah — good solid native timber that is hardwearing

Merbau and **Batu** — from Asia and cheaper than Australian timbers, pest resistant and durable in a red-brown colour

Treated Pine — pale colour but can be stained and is an inexpensive option

Spotted Gum — a dark timber that is pest and bushfire resistant

Ironbark — very durable in a red or grey colour

Tallow — very durable in a yellowish colour

River Red Gum — durable in a pale red colour

Pool fencing

Fencing around a pool saves kids from drowning so they are mandatory. If your pool fencing is absent or inadequate, you will receive heavy fines from your local council. Although mandatory, fencing can still add ambience to the pool area. This is where a pool designer can add style to the area.

Fencing needs to comply with the following standards:

- No gaps to squeeze through

- No climbing holds

- At least 1.2 m high

- Strong enough so that a child cannot force open.

Aluminium and **steel** fences have upright bars with upper and lower rails. There are various designs in this style of fencing. **Safety glass** fencing is the most expensive but looks fantastic. They can be frameless and less obtrusive than most other fences.

Pool lighting

Lighting in and around the pool is essential to create a stunning atmosphere. There is nothing quite like an illuminated pool to dazzle your guests! There are many options and your pool designer will help you decide. You need to consider your budget, of course, and whether to have **LED** (more expensive) or **incandescent** (cheaper) lights, or an energy efficient option. The colour of your tiles will affect the diffused colour when lighting is added. Depending on the size of your pool, one or two underwater lights are adequate, and you can add light from a number of sources around the pool area and in the garden to soften the effect. **Fibre optic** lighting is more expensive than LED but you can produce wonderful light shows.

Solar lights can also add a dimension to your lighting when used with other forms of lighting.

Water features

When choosing the design of your pool, you should talk to your pool designer about factoring in a water feature.

There are so many options which are only limited by the imagination. The water feature can add a new dimension to any pool by adding movement and sound effects. The many types of water features include:

Rock waterfalls (water cascades over rocks), **sheetfalls** (sheet of water flows over a surface), **laminar jets** (steady stream of water), **fountains, raised walls** where water pours out of statues, **fountain bubblers, jets, infinity edge overflow falls**, and **elevated ripple effects**.

Most water features run off the primary pool pump. Also consider the type of lighting you require around the water feature.

Pool covers

It is a statutory requirement in Australia for council approval, that a solar blanket is installed in all new pools.

Here are other reasons to have a pool cover:

- Reduces the amount of leaves and branches dropping into the pool

- Needs less vacuuming

- Slows down evaporation so you don't need to refill or top up the water in your pool so often

- Reduces the pool's chemical consumption and hence, the chemical reactions by the body

- Helps retain heat.

Unsightly pool covers and rollers can be concealed under the paving.

Alfrescos

Alfresco areas provide the ability to live both inside and outside at the same time by having doors that open onto the outdoor area. Having an outdoor seating area will add useability to the pool area. Think about how you want to use this area and how many people you may need to accommodate for seating or other activities. The pool designer will see that it merges seamlessly with the design and construction of the pool and your home.

Q5. How do I know if it's a fair price?

The swimming pool construction business is so individual that it is impossible to give clients an actual cost without having a site visit. Once the pool designer can see the space and size, and any potential challenges in the site, he can start to think about a plan that will allow all the customer requirements to be met. The cost will depend on the size and accessibility of your site, the materials used, the intricacy of the work, and any other landscaping or structures required. The budget for building a swimming pool can be suited to your requirements with negotiation.

We recommend an inground concrete swimming pool because you get a personalised pool for your environment and one that you will enjoy for many years to come. There is ongoing maintenance, of course, but if good-quality materials have been used in the construction of the pool, the maintenance will be manageable. With good design and construction, this kind of pool looks stunning and is unbeatable in quality. An inground concrete swimming pool will also add considerable value to your home, its liveability and its eventual saleability.

Top 4 considerations regarding price

1. Size and space

Large and small spaces each have their own challenges. Two acres of blank canvas is an amazing opportunity when the owner has asked for a Bali resort in their backyard! It is a challenge because it's a massive area to fill with all the elements that make up a stunning resort.

This is, of course, the top end with regard to price as the bigger the size, the more materials and time required. If the space is smaller, the price is smaller because of the smaller about of materials and less time taken to complete the project.

Smaller areas have challenges with regard to creating a resort feel in a limited space.

2. Accessibility

If it is very difficult to access the area where your pool is being built, this will have ramifications on cost. If you have a small space, the challenge is to be able to work with the myriad equipment that is required to get the job done. You can still have many of the elements of a large pool such as decking, outdoor entertaining area, pergola, and a swim-up bar. The challenge is to fit it all into a workable and attractive design. Other difficult locations are on the edges of cliffs, with infinity-edge (or vanishing edge) pools. Some suburban properties may be subdivided and have difficult access to the back of the property.

All this increases the time, and consequently, the cost of the pool.

3. Materials

The best quality and longest lasting products are obviously more expensive. There are always options to choose products for different budgets, however. The swimming pool is a harsh environment, subject to all sorts of forces. Wherever health and water is concerned, the utmost care must be taken with hygiene and cleanliness. Top-quality products are durable, reliable, strong, easy to use, resistant to corrosion and have warranties.

4. Complexity of design

Most clients would love the whole menu: the lagoon or resort swimming pool, swim-up bar, timber decking, outdoor entertaining area with outdoor kitchen, a water feature, top-of-the-range fencing, luxuriant jungle garden, easy-to-maintain landscaping, Bali daybed or meditation room — the list is abundant.

All of these features create an amazing environment for your pool and obviously add to the time and design specifications of the job. The more complex the design, the more materials are required and the more time and labour is needed to complete the work. These are all elements to keep in mind when requesting a quote.

Other tips

- Have a detailed quote including the scope of works, what's included and what is not
- Get everything in writing before construction begins.

Ask about other potential costs. Be aware that changing your mind and amending the design or anything about the contract after you have agreed will result in extra cost for you, extra time and effort for the pool designer, and potential issues over time. To ensure this does not happen, be very sure and decide on everything before you sign the contract or approve the final design.

A pool for all seasons

No matter what the season, whether the summer is just coming to an end, or the mornings are just about to warm up, you need to start thinking about how you are going to stay cool before the heat penetrates your life.

There is no doubt that a beautiful concrete swimming pool is a major investment. In the long term, that beautiful lagoon with decking and fabulous entertainment area is going to add the same value and more to the home that you love, and will be an inviting place for friends and family to gather. Even if you're not thinking of selling for some time, your swimming pool is a worthwhile addition to your home.

A beautifully designed concrete pool that offers quality construction and aesthetic landscaping of the outdoor area complements the property and creates a wonderful environment in which to live. If the pool has the correct safety requirements, it is a great incentive to teach your children to swim, and they can enjoy many great times in the pool.

That's it!

We hope that you have found this **Concrete Pool Buyers' Guide** informative and that it will help you with your options when you decide to buy a pool.

You may also find some of these links helpful in your search. Just go to our website at www.thewatersedge.com.au.

Good luck in your search.

About The Water's Edge

The Water's Edge is a family-owned swimming pool construction business that specialises in building individual and unique swimming pools and landscapes. We design and build pools, alfresco areas, landscapes and outdoor entertainment areas to suit your lifestyle, with a particular specialty towards unusually shaped areas or difficult sites.

The Water's Edge is a member of the Housing Industry Association Ltd (HIA) and the Swimming Pool & Spa Association of Western Australia (SPASA). The company has won many awards for its designs.

Steve Nener, Director/Pool Designer

Steve has been working in the swimming pool industry for more than 30 years. He is a qualified carpenter and has skills and experience in carpentry, project management, landscaping, building and construction, renovation, logistics, holistic design, team leadership, estimating and supply management. Steve's main goal is to provide flexible lifestyle, landscape design and poolside living choices that make people happy in their home environments.

Robin Bower, Communications Manager

Robin manages the social media platforms, writes blog articles and updates the website. She is an author and accredited editor with more than 20 years publishing experience in Australia and overseas. She has had almost 50 articles published in publications based in Hong Kong, Perth and Melbourne, and was awarded her Master of Creative Writing from the University of Canberra. See her other work at www.robinbower.com.au.

If you would like to join our mailing list to receive helpful tips on all aspects of buying, owning and maintaining a pool, please sign up at our website.

Other ways to connect with The Water's Edge:

Website | Facebook | Twitter

Instagram | Google+ | LinkedIn

Notes